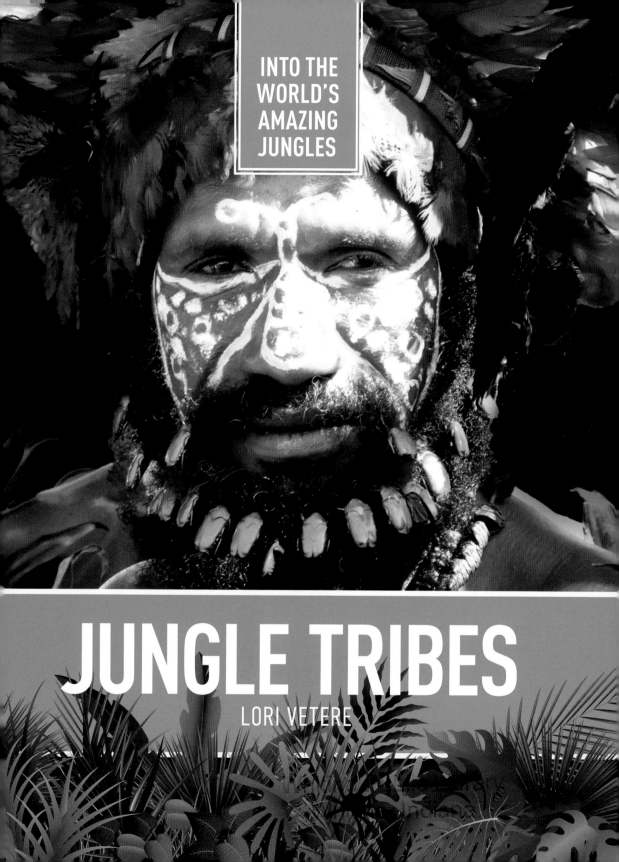

INTO THE
WORLD'S
AMAZING
JUNGLES

JUNGLE TRIBES

LORI VETERE

INTO THE WORLD'S AMAZING JUNGLES

Jungle Bugs & Vegetation

Jungle Facts & Figures

Jungle Tribes

Jungle Wildlife

INTO THE WORLD'S AMAZING JUNGLES

JUNGLE TRIBES

LORI VETERE

MASON CREST

Mason Crest
450 Parkway Drive, Suite D
Broomall, Pennsylvania 19008
(866) MCP-BOOK (toll-free)
www.masoncrest.com

First printing
9 8 7 6 5 4 3 2 1

ISBN (hardback) 978-1-4222-4095-3
ISBN (series) 978-1-4222-4092-2
ISBN (ebook) 978-1-4222-7704-1

Cataloging-in-Publication Data on file with the Library of Congress

Developed and Produced by National Highlights Inc.
Editor: Andrew Luke
Interior and cover design: Jana Rade, impact studios
Production: Michelle Luke

QR CODES AND LINKS TO THIRD-PARTY CONTENT

You may gain access to certain third-party content ("Third-Party Sites") by scanning and using the QR Codes that appear in this publication (the "QR Codes"). We do not operate or control in any respect any information, products, or services on such Third-Party Sites linked to by us via the QR Codes included in this publication, and we assume no responsibility for any materials you may access using the QR Codes. Your use of the QR Codes may be subject to terms, limitations, or restrictions set forth in the applicable terms of use or otherwise established by the owners of the Third-Party Sites. Our linking to such Third-Party Sites via the QR Codes does not imply an endorsement or sponsorship of such Third-Party Sites or the information, products, or services offered on or through the Third-Party Sites, nor does it imply an endorsement or sponsorship of this publication by the owners of such Third-Party Sites.

CONTENTS

Introduction. 8

CHAPTER 1. The Tribes 11

CHAPTER 2. First Contact 23

CHAPTER 3. Looking Back and Ahead 35

CHAPTER 4. A Tribal Way of Life 47

CHAPTER 5. The Dangers of the Modern
World. 59

Series Glossary of Key Terms 70

Documentaries 72

Resources. 73

Index. 76

About the Author. 80

KEY ICONS TO LOOK FOR:

Words to Understand: These words with their easy-to-understand definitions will increase the reader's understanding of the text while building vocabulary skills.

Sidebars: This boxed material within the main text allows readers to build knowledge, gain insights, explore possibilities, and broaden their perspectives by weaving together additional information to provide realistic and holistic perspectives.

Educational Videos: Readers can view videos by scanning our QR codes, providing them with additional educational content to supplement the text. Examples include news coverage, moments in history, speeches, iconic sports moments and much more!

Text-Dependent Questions: These questions send the reader back to the text for more careful attention to the evidence presented there.

Research Projects Readers are pointed toward areas of further inquiry connected to each chapter. Suggestions are provided for projects that encourage deeper research and analysis.

Series Glossary of Key Terms: This back-of-the book glossary contains terminology used throughout this series. Words found here increase the reader's ability to read and comprehend higher-level books and articles in this field.

THE CONGO

Area – 687,000 m² (1,780,000 km²).

Home to: Aka tribes, Forest Leopards, Raffia Palms.

This jungle is the basin of the Congo river, covering the northern half of the Democratic Republic of the Congo and spreading west toward the Atlantic Ocean through five other countries.

More than 400 species of mammals, 700 species of fish, and 1,000 species of birds are found here.

THE AMAZON

Area – 2,123,000 m² (5,500,000 km²).

Home to: Tribes of Acre, Giant Otters, Rubber trees.

About half of the world's biggest jungle is located in Brazil. The other half spreads into eight other South American countries.

The Amazon contains 20% of all the freshwater in the world.

SUNDARBANS RESERVE

Area – 4000 m^2 (10,000 km^2).

Home to: Bengal Tigers.

This region lies mostly in Bangladesh and spreads to the west into India.

The Sundarbans was declared a UNESCO World Heritage Site in 1997.

PAPUA NEW GUINEA

Area – 116,000 m^2 (300,000 km^2).

Home to: Huli tribes, Tree Kangaroos, Blue Marble trees.

The eastern half of the island of New Guinea is the country known as Papua New Guinea and was once almost completely covered by jungle. Since 1972, more than 80,000 km^2, or more than 20 percent, has been cleared.

BORNEO LOWLAND

Area – 165,000 m^2 (427,500 km2).

Home to: Penan tribes, Proboscis Monkeys, Asian Tiger Mosquitos.

This jungle encompasses the entire island of Borneo, which is shared by Brunei, Malaysia and Indonesia,

In Borneo, 700 tree species were once discovered in just 25 acres (0.1 km^2).

We live in a world of technology, a vast world that is interconnected in a great variety of ways—through the internet, cell phones, television, radio, oral history, and the printed word. Most of us live in or near large urban centers and assume that most of the world's civilizations are very similar to ours. What many of us city dwellers forget is that there remain indigenous jungle peoples around the globe who live very different lives than we do. Hundreds of these tribes share the Earth with us, and the more that we learn about them, the more important it becomes to protect their rights and advocate for their fair treatment. They range from peoples who are fully assimilated into the neighboring civilization to a few tribes that are still completely wild.

This book will introduce you to four different jungle tribes who live in four distinct regions of the world. Each of the tribes live in the world's largest jungles, and each tribe has been chosen because of its unique and interesting history. The main tribes we will discuss include the Brazilian Amazon region's Acre Tribes, Papua

New Guinea's Huli Wigmen, Central Africa's Aka people (also known as the Mbenga), and the Penan people of the Sarawak state in Borneo. We will also mention some of the other jungle tribes existing in our world today along the way.

Some of these tribes have had limited contact with the rest of the world, and one of these groups of people can still be referred to as one of the estimated one hundred uncontacted tribes. Uncontacted tribes may have chosen to live in voluntary isolation for a number of reasons, although many governments and corporations do not want to respect these tribes' right to self-determination.

The modern world holds many dangers and threats for these tribes. Have they lost their homes because of deforestation or mining practices nearby? Have they suffered from coming into contact with modern diseases? Have they lost their unique culture because of assimilation or contact with the mainstream world? These are some of the challenges for these people who have been forced to face the harsh realities of a changing planet.

WORDS TO UNDERSTAND

amalgamation – the action of merging or uniting two or more separate things

indigenous – living, growing, or occurring naturally in a particular country or region

nomadic – the life of a nomad or wanderer who has no permanent home, and moves from one place to another frequently

pith – the spongy, soft tissue inside both plants and animals

tajem – a poison made from milky tree latex which causes a prey's heart to stop functioning

CHAPTER 1

The Tribes

TRIBES OF ACRE
(BRAZILIAN AMAZON REGION)

The first tribe we will study is located in the westernmost Brazilian state of Acre. According to Fundação Nacional do Índio (FUNAI), the agency in Brazil responsible for **indigenous** affairs, there are between twenty-seven and eighty separate indigenous groups who live in extreme remoteness in the vast region of the Amazon. This region is so large and wild that it has the greatest number of tribes that have never been contacted existing in the world today. An unauthorized flight in March 2014 took pictures of a group, first spotted in 2008 shooting arrows at an airplane after it also illegally flew over their territory. Brazilian authorities were angry that the flight occurred since the government is trying to protect the tribes in Acre from interference from the mainstream world. There are accounts, however, that some of these uncontacted tribes are raiding other communities that have been contacted by the modern world and are stealing industrial items like machetes, axes, clothing, and aluminum pots from the contacted villagers.

A tribal village on the bank of the Amazon river in Brazil.

The fact that tribes in Acre still exist that have had little or no contact with the modern world has been denied many times by oil companies who are determined to exploit the jungle, gold miners, logging companies who only care about profits and aren't concerned about deforestation, large agricultural companies, some members of the Brazilian government, and cattle ranchers. Despite the great number of people who are determined to move the tribes people of Acre at any cost, as of 2017 there are reported to be at least four distinct uncontacted tribes, with a total of about six hundred people, still living deep in Acre's tropical jungle.

In May of 2017, the leader of one of the state of Acre's largest groups appealed for help to protect the lands of his tribe. Chief Tashka Yawanawa says his people need protection from the Brazilian government because its new policies threaten the tribe's land rights. At an event organized to appeal to the international community on behalf of the Yawanawa people, the chief said, "It's a time of struggle for indigenous people … We are losing [our] rights, especially about land…This new government is controlled by agribusiness and the intention is to exploit our territory for logging, mining, getting minerals. If the land is taken away … it will be genocide for indigenous people." Unfortunately, this story is an example of the norm rather than the exception for indigenous people and their land around the world.

HULI WIGMEN (PAPUA NEW GUINEA)

The second tribe that we will be studying is the Huli Wigmen of Papua New Guinea. When European explorers first entered the vast Highland area of Papua New Guinea during the 1930s, they were amazed to discover more than one million people living there in a completely undeveloped region. The largest ethnic group currently living in the Highlands of Tari are the Huli, who number between three hundred thousand and four hundred thousand people. The men of Huli have a very colorful tradition of wearing elaborately decorated woven wigs, which they adorn with bunches of multi-colored feathers whenever they have a celebratory festival. A unique clan, the Huli Wigmen live apart from Highland civilization, and teach boys, who are sent to them at fourteen or fifteen years of age, how to make these colorful wigs. Boys usually stay with the Wigmen for about ten years, learning to collect feathers, make armbands, and grow the hair necessary to create these complex and highly wrought wigs.

Modern Hulis stage elaborate shows in full traditional costume at local tribe festivals.

Nowadays, only the oldest men wear their traditional costumes every day. But every man puts on his traditional costume and wig on special occasions. Hulis celebrate many festivals and seasonal events when tourists and other visitors can see them dressed in their elaborate makeup and ceremonial wigs. These men are a sight to see when they are decorated with flowers and clay, bones, bird feathers, hand-woven fabrics, plant oils, shells, and precious stones. Watching the Huli Wigmen dance their Bird Dance, which copies the ways of birds-of-paradise, is really an unforgettable experience.

The traditions of the Huli Wigmen are still strong, but only the Huli that live in the most remote areas of Papua New Guinea still follow the time-honored lifestyle of the tribe. This means that they constantly engage in skirmishes with their neighbors, usually about women, land, and pigs. When a Huli is injured, they prefer to seek vengeance, and vengeance includes stealing the pigs of their foes. Pigs are a great symbol of wealth for these tribesmen. They are not eaten. Instead, they serve as money and are used to buy brides, make ritual payments, and are used as insurance payments if a tribe member has died or been severely injured.

AKA OF CENTRAL AFRICA

The Aka, also known as the Bayaka, are a **nomadic** people, descended from the Mbenga pygmy people who live in the southwestern part of the Congo known as the Central African Republic, and also in the Congo's Brazzaville region. This tribe is a long established hunter-gatherer tribe. Their diet is very rich. They eat 28 different species of game, 63 plants, 20 different insect species, in addition to fruit, nuts, mushrooms, honey, and roots. Their history is rich and includes an **amalgamation** with several other tribes who moved into the Aka territory to avoid being caught by slave traders in the 1700s. They

The Aka are a traditional hunter-gatherer tribe. The use of nets is a modern Aka hunting technique.

A Few Interesting Facts About Jungle Tribes

Most of the world's isolated jungle tribes live in the Amazon Jungle, in the border area between Brazil and Peru. Both legal and illegal companies that practice logging and mining all around them have threatened their way of life for years. Large areas of the jungle around them are also being destroyed by the practice of slash-and-burn farming, where mainstream-world farmers burn the forest and use the ashes as fertilizer to grow crops like soy.

Tribe members in Acre use giant bows and arrows to hunt their prey. They also love to eat tortoises. Large mounds of turtle shells have been left behind in a number of abandoned camps.

became elephant hunters to trade tusks for the outside civilization's ivory trade. They were forced to work on rubber plantations in the early part of the twentieth century by the colonialists in French Equatorial Africa. Many of them escaped into the jungle, only to be forced to find employment in the coffee plantations of their neighbors for economic reasons. The Aka are famous for their oral traditions and their complex music.

The Aka are thought to be the first inhabitants of Central Africa. A very interesting fact about Aka men is that they are so nurturing that they have been called the best fathers in the world. They are either holding their children or within arm's reach of them approximately 47% of the time, much more than any other fathers in the world! Aka men are also nonviolent toward women. In Aka societies, it is the traditional role of the women to use threats and intimidation towards men when they "misbehave."

Akas are traditionally good hunters, known for their ability to find red hogs, duikers (small African antelopes), chimpanzees, squirrels, and birds. They are also

Huli Wigmen of New Guineas live mostly on sweet potatoes and jungle greens. They rarely eat meat—only on special occasions. They raise a lot of pigs, but pigs are used for currency and to show wealth. The pigs are used to buy land and are only eaten on very special occasions.

The Aka tribe of Central Africa are better known in the United States as pygmies. This term is now considered disrespectful, and anthropologists are recommending that it be replaced with a phrase like "tropical forest forager."

The Penan of Borneo are a soft spoken people who give respect to their elders and have what is known as a headman; however, they are a very communal tribe and share everything equally among all tribe members.

Take a look at an example of how life has changed for the Penan.

excellent foragers, which means that they are skilled at finding edible plants in the tropical rainforest. It is a sad fact that today the vast majority of Aka tribes people are not allowed to live their traditional lifestyle. The area of Africa where they live has been populated with Europeans and other outsiders who have taken over the land and made enormous coffee plantations. The Akas must earn money by either working in these plantations or by working for large lumber companies.

THE PENAN (SARAWAK, BORNEO)

The last tribe that we will study is the Penan people of Sarawak in Borneo. These tropical rainforest dwellers have lived for thousands of years as nomadic hunter-gatherers. Although a small percentage of the tribe are still nomads, the majority of the people settled down in villages during the 1960s. The Penan are skilled hunters and hunt for wild boar, lizards, squirrels, and many other small animals, including barking deer, using blowpipes dipped in **tajem** for their weapons. The jungle that they live in has one of Earth's largest varieties of plants, fruiting trees, and different types of aromatic woods. The Penan's main source of carbohydrates comes from the wild sago palm's starchy **pith**. Both the nomadic part of the tribe and the villagers rely heavily on the jungle for all of their needs. Unfortunately, their way of life is being threatened by the continued destruction of the jungle by commercial loggers who have had the permission of the government since the 1970s.

Traditionally the Penan hunter-gatherers followed a practice called "molong" which means that a person should never take more than they need to survive. They used every part of the plants they gathered, either for food or as medicine. In the same manner, they used all the parts of the animals they hunted—the fur, skin, and hides, and other parts for shelter and clothing—besides using the meat for food. Of course, this practice is in stark contrast with the practices of the loggers and outsiders who encroached on the land of the Penan and destroyed much of the jungle by over-harvesting, polluting, and setting up huge palm oil and rubber plantations.

RESEARCH PROJECT

Choose a rainforest or jungle that is located in the Amazon region of Brazil, Papua New Guinea, Central Africa, or Borneo. Find out what types of plants and trees are found in the rain forest. Then write a paper discussing one or more of these plants and trees, and discuss how they are used—in nutrition, medicine, construction, etc.

Traditionally a hunter-gatherer people, the Penan are skilled at catching everything from fish to boar and use every part of each plant and animal they take from the jungle.

The younger generations of Penan now make their homes in permanent settlements and have adopted year-round farming, mostly because the sago palms were lost or destroyed, and the jungle was damaged by pollution, causing there to be a scarcity of deer, wild boar, and other game. It is estimated that currently only some 200 members of the Penan tribe still practice a nomadic lifestyle. Activists among the Penan and outside environmentalists continue to fight against the government-sponsored acacia and palm oil plantations and giant hydroelectric projects by making road blockades and speaking out to the world press.

These four tribes will be our primary focus, but we will also introduce many other groups from various jungles around the world with unique and interesting stories and experiences that complement the discussion throughout the book.

TEXT-DEPENDENT QUESTIONS

1. What kinds of animals do the Penan of Sarawak in Borneo hunt? And what kind of weapons do they use?
2. What is the diet of the Aka of Central Africa?
3. What role do pigs play in the culture of the Huli Wigmen of Papua New Guinea?

WORDS TO UNDERSTAND

colonialists – persons who impose control or governing influence of a nation over a dependent country, territory, or people

constraints – something that controls or limits what a person is able to do

diphtheria – a very contagious bacterial disease that may cause fatal nerve and heart damage; it is rare in more developed countries because of immunizations

unscrupulous – dishonest or unfair, showing or having no moral principles

CHAPTER 2

First Contact

HULI TRIBE (PAPUA NEW GUINEA)

The Huli tribe and other indigenous groups have lived in the central highlands of Papua New Guinea for more than a thousand years. The mainstream world did not know of the existence of the Huli Wigmen and other Papua New Guinean tribes until the early 1930s, when Dan and Mick Leahy, two brothers (gold prospectors from Australia), arrived with a large group of coastal tribesmen and other Australians to search for gold. This group of foreigners was as astounded to meet the inland tribes as the tribes were to meet them. Soon afterward, planes arrived with equipment and supplies to the great astonishment of the natives. A lot of trading took place—mostly shells, beads, and axes in exchange for food.

After this first contact with the Huli and other tribes, **unscrupulous** treasure seekers infiltrated the land, looking for gold. One shameful moment in history occurred when a group of gold prospectors, led by two brothers, Tom and Jack Fox, decided to take food from the natives without trading for it and brutally killed anyone who objected (it is said that fifty tribespeople were shot and killed in one day). When the Fox brothers

Gold prospectors from Australia were the first to contact the Huli in the 1930s.

returned home to Australia, they tried to suppress all knowledge of what they did. It was not until many years later that historical researchers retraced the steps of the brothers, interviewed some tribesmen who had met them, and discovered what they had done. Unfortunately, history books seldom recorded this kind of event since actions of this kind were very common.

AKA TRIBE (CENTRAL AFRICA)

There is evidence to suggest that human beings have inhabited Central Africa's western forests and jungles for more than thirty thousand years. Among the oldest inhabitants of the equatorial jungle are an ethnic group characterized by short stature (adults are less than five feet tall). The Aka tribe belongs to this ethnic group, and because of their gentleness, their preference for remaining as hunter-gatherers instead of becoming farmers, and their shorter height, the Aka have suffered for hundreds of years from ethnic violence, discrimination, and slavery.

Georg August Schweinfurth (1836–1925) was a well-known Baltic German botanist who was the first European to document contact with the Aka in 1870.

Welsh journalist Henry Morton Stanley (1841–1904) labeled the Aka, "pygmies of Darkest Africa" in 1891.

Historical records show that various explorers of Central Africa took captives of the tribe and brought them to Europe and other parts of Africa. In 2300 B.C., Pharaoh Phiops II wrote of a Bayaka dancer who had been brought back from a jungle expedition. Greek philosopher Aristotle (ca. 340 B.C.) and historian Herodotus (ca. 400 B.C.) talked about the Bayaka people. Records stop there, until 1870, when a man named Georg Schweinfurth became the first European to document contact with the Aka. Two explorers, Henry Morton Stanley (1891) and Giovanni Miani (1880) were also instrumental in publicizing the existence of these tribes (Stanley called them the "pygmies of Darkest Africa"). The lives of the Akas were changed drastically after these "rediscoveries" and European **colonialists** soon forced them into slavery.

INDIGENOUS TRIBES OF ACRE, BRAZILIAN AMAZON REGION

The westernmost state of Acre in Brazil is home to a number of jungle tribes that have had very little contact with the mainstream world and continue to live a life free from the **constraints** of modern civilization. One tribe, the Xatanawa, was said to be observed since 2008, but not contacted until June of 2014 by members of FUNAI.

The group that was contacted are a subgroup of the Asháninka called the Macaw People, or Xatanawa. Some members of this group appeared at the side of a river close to the edge of the jungle and called to people in boats, making gestures that looked like they were asking for food and for help. FUNAI took a few interpreters with them to meet up with this group the second time that they appeared in late June 2014. Fortunately, the interpreters were able to speak with the men and discovered that they made contact because they needed allies and weapons. They told the interpreters that either drug traffickers or illegal loggers had come into their village, and shot and killed many of their elders. There were also stories that their huts had been set on fire. After the invasion, many of the native people became sick with diphtheria and the flu, because they did not have any immunity to fight off these illnesses.

MASHCO PIRO TRIBE (AMAZON, PERU)

The Mashco Piro tribe (also known as Nomole and the Cujareño people) have lived in isolation for many years in Peru's Amazonian jungle. They first came to the attention of the mainstream world during the late 1800s, when rubber plantation owners who had encroached on their territory enslaved many of them. They managed to escape from the slavers and rebuffed the efforts of missionaries who were in the area. Since that time, the six hundred to eight hundred Mashco Piro people kept to themselves, but have had irregular contact with other settled tribes in the area for the last forty years.

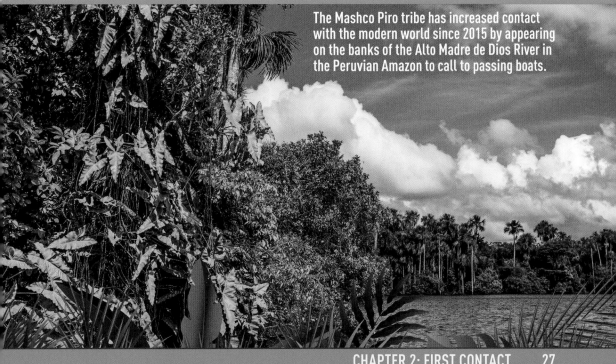

The Mashco Piro tribe has increased contact with the modern world since 2015 by appearing on the banks of the Alto Madre de Dios River in the Peruvian Amazon to call to passing boats.

Since 2015, the Mashco have been increasing contact with the mainstream world. They appear on the river bank and call out to boats to give them clothing, food, machetes, axes, etc. They have also increased their aggression toward other neighboring tribes, entering other tribes' villages, stealing food and other items, and even using bows and arrows to attack and even kill people from other tribes. The situation has become very dangerous and has led to the government of Peru evacuating two nearby villages and patrolling the Alto Madre de Dios River daily.

PACAHUARA TRIBE (BOLIVIA)

The Pacahuara people are one of the primary indigenous groups of Bolivia. They lived in northern Bolivia in Pando, a region between Rio Madre De Dios to the south and the border of Brazil to the north, spoke an unwritten language and practiced a harvesting-based and agricultural lifestyle. They grew corn, rice, cassava (also known as yucca or manioc) and bananas, and traded palm hearts and chestnuts with other isolated jungle tribes. They also survived by hunting and fishing.

Before the rubber industry and logging industry invaded the Amazon region and made slaves out of the people, it is estimated that more than 40,000 Pacahuaras lived in the jungle. These industries, in the space of just 200 years, destroyed their land, forcefully displaced them from their original homes, and killed many of their tribe. Only a few Pacahuaras were able to escape the toll of war and starvation by fleeing into the remotest parts of the jungle. By 1969 only a handful of them were still alive.

Between 1969 and 1971 a non-profit Christian group called the Summer Institute of Linguistics (SIL International) decided to help the small group of Pacahuaras that remained (it is reported that there is still one uncontacted group of Pacahuara left, still living in the Pando region of Bolivia), with the stated intention of having them join a group of people

The Pacahuara tribe of northern Bolivia grew yucca plants with edible roots among several other crops.

who spoke a related language. SIL has been criticized by many indigenous right activists and anthropologists for creating conflicts among the tribes people by changing their culture, studying their languages to convert them and write a Bible in their language, and having mostly negative influences inside the communities where they work. However, in this instance, it appears that they rescued this family from almost certain death.

In the case of these Pacahuara people, a man, his two sister wives, and their seven children were moved out of their original lands to a town called Puerto Tujuré in the territory of the Chácobo. Reports of the fate of this family have emerged since 1974. Of the original seven siblings five married and had children. In total, forty-three people have descended from this original family so far, including seven people who have since passed away.

A Few Interesting Facts About First Contact With Tribes

The Sentinelese Tribe

Living on North Sentinel Island (belonging to the Andaman Islands) in the Bay of Bengal is an isolated tribe called the Sentinelese. These tribespeople have warded off visits from sailors and other adventurers for hundreds of years and have acted so menacingly that people who were repelled from visiting have reported that the tribespeople were cannibals. The first person to make peaceful contact with this tribe was Trilokinath Pandit, an official of the Indian government, in 1991. The island is owned by India, and the Indian government landed on the island twice in 2001 to take a census. About seventy Sentinelese were counted. In 1997, the government decided to adopt a "hands-off and eyes-on" policy with the islands, which means that they do not land there, and they monitor their territory by air, and patrol the ocean by boat, so that no poachers or other unwanted people will be able to land.

Bose Yacu, one of the original children who was moved to the Chácobo territory was interviewed in 2013. She stated that she was grateful for the move because the Chácobo welcomed them with open arms and the Pacahuara assimilated into the tribe and learned their language and culture. On December 31, 2016, it was reported that one of the 5 remaining original Pacahuara, a 57 year old woman, had died in Puerto Tujuré, Bolivia, leaving only 4 original members who can only recall a few songs that their father sang in the Pacahuara language.

The Ruc Tribe

The Ruc tribe live in the jungles of Vietnam. North Vietnamese soldiers first encountered them during the Vietnam War when they were hiding supplies in the jungle of what is currently known as Phong Nha-Ke Bang National Park in 1959. Many attempts to relocate this tribe by the Vietnamese government have met with little success. The Rucs have occasionally agreed to be resettled on farmlands, but as soon as they can, they return to the jungle, where they live in caves.

Other Papua New Guinean Tribes

Besides the Huli, there are other tribes that have only had a little contact with government authorities, anthropologists, scientists, etc. in Papua New Guinea. These tribes live deep in the jungle, and there are few facts known about them, aside from their name. Here are a few of the names of the mostly uncontacted tribes: Gusawi, Kokiri, Langguru, Teriku, Derewo, Manu, Foja, Waruta, and Brazza-Digul. It is thought that these tribes are pre-literate.

The Ruc tribe was first discovered in the 1950s living in the jungles of what is now Phong Nha Ke Bang National Park in Vietnam.

Very little is known about the so-called Sentinelese people, who live in isolation in the Indian Ocean .

UNCONTACTED TRIBES LEFT IN THE WORLD

For a variety of reasons, there are less than fifty small groups of people around the world that are still listed as "uncontacted." These tribes have had limited contact with others in the past, especially with other isolated tribes. Many of them came into contact with rubber plantation owners, loggers, gold miners, and oil workers either at the end of the nineteenth century or throughout the twentieth century. These contacts were violent at times; and many tribesmen were massacred by corporations that wanted their land or to enslave them or individuals who wanted to trade or take advantage of them. Missionaries have also frequently traveled to remote areas of the world in order to bring their particular religion to the "savages." These types of actions caused the uncontacted tribes to run away and hide in the most remote parts of the jungle.

Sometimes these tribes develop diseases from coming into contact with people from the mainstream world causing many deaths. This was the case when the Spanish conquistadors led by Francisco Pizarro met up with the Incas in Peru in the early 1530s, and when Hernán Cortés and his men met up with the Aztecs in Mexico in 1519. More than two hundred thousand Aztecs died after being invaded by the Spanish colonists, who brought diseases like smallpox, measles, and mumps with them. About the same number of Incas were also killed by diseases. Is it any wonder, then, that some tribes prefer to hide far away from "civilized" man?

RESEARCH PROJECT

Research and choose three other tribes, each from different parts of the world, and write a paper discussing these groups and the challenges they each face to maintain its particular way of life.

TEXT-DEPENDENT QUESTIONS

1. Why did the Asháninka tribe decide to make contact with FUNAI (the National Indigenous Foundation of Brazil)?
2. What were the Leahy brothers searching for when they entered the territory of the Huli in Papua New Guinea in the early 1930s? How did they act when they met the tribespeople?
3. Who were some of the first historical figures who wrote about or transported some of the Bayaka people to their land?

WORDS TO UNDERSTAND

cassowary – large flightless bird native to New Guinea that is in the same family as emus

pièce de résistance – the most important or exciting thing or event (borrowed from the French)

quarantine – a period of isolation in which people that have been exposed to contagious or infectious diseases are placed in an area where no one else can enter

CHAPTER 3

Looking Back And Ahead

HULI WIGMEN (TARI, PAPUA NEW GUINEA)

It's been almost ninety years since Mick Leahy, his brother, and a group of outsiders trekked into the central highlands of Papua New Guinea looking for gold and instead discovered approximately a million people who wore loincloths and colorful headdresses and carried bows and arrows! The films that were taken at the time show a wild side to the Huli, who frequently fought each other holding huge shields and brandishing giant clubs.

Although traditional clan warfare still exists to this day, it is done less often, since some of the Huli have been able to buy guns from mainstream peoples and fights are more deadly. The Huli have assimilated well into the modern world, even though those old tribal conflicts still erupt.   They have adapted their love of tribal get-togethers and personal decoration into performances at large festivals called sing-sings held every August and September in Goroka and Mount Hagen. Thousands of visitors come to watch the Huli act out their traditional myths and legends, wearing their vividly colorful feathers, leaf aprons that cover their backsides, a feather of a **cassowary** through their nose, bright yellow body makeup, and the **pièce de résistance**—their fabulous large, mushroom-shaped wigs, grown especially for these performances by a dedicated group of tribesmen called the Huli Wigmen.

Of course, this display of costumes, dancing, and oral tradition are now reserved for festival seasons. Most of the Huli now dress in traditional Western clothes—only the very oldest of the men still dress in the way of their ancestors. Although they still use the traditional ways of agriculture, they have incorporated modern knives and cooking utensils into their lives.

HULI TRADITION

The Huli are masters of oral tradition, by which they pass on the words and ideas of their ancestors. When white men first entered their lands in the early 1930s, many Huli thought that they were descendents of Tahoname, who was the white son of Tagonimabe, the very first man, who left Papua New Guinea and thought to be immortal. That's why some Huli welcomed the explorers, gave them food, and escorted them around the territory. Some Huli were more wary and would not let the white men touch them or accept their gifts. Their distrust was justified when, after a large group of Huli had surrounded the explorers, shots were fired by the white men and two Huli were killed.

Tree kangaroos are among the favorite prey of the few Huli tribesmen who still hunt for their own food.

Displays of traditional costumes and dancing now take place mostly during festival season.

LOOKING AHEAD

A great change has come over the lives of the Huli in the last twenty years since natural gas and minerals have been discovered on their land. An increase in wealth has drastically altered the lives of more modern thinking Huli, and it is said that many Huli have been catapulted headlong into the hectic world of the twenty-first century. Some Huli men have established businesses all through Papua New Guinea. Huli men still hunt for meat, especially birds, tree kangaroos, and possums, but they have added homemade shotguns to their traditional bows and arrows. Huli women are great farmers, and have introduced many new crops into the Huli diet, such as sweet potatoes, cabbage, and corn.

AKA TRIBE (CENTRAL AFRICA)

When Georg Schweinfurth "rediscovered" the Aka tribe in 1870, it opened up a time of dramatic change for the Aka. Before that time, the Aka (also known as Bayaka, Ba'aka or Baka) spent all of their time hunting and foraging in the tropical jungle regions of what was then known as the Congo. A great demand for ivory rose in the last part of the nineteenth century in the mainstream world, and the Aka became the principal providers of this ivory to the colonial traders. Aka tribesmen killed elephants with spears and even guns until the elephant population in that area was depleted.

In the 1930s, the French colonial government tried to force the Aka out of their traditional jungle villages and onto farms.

Aka tribeswomen are joyous at the conclusion of a successful hunt.

During the period between 1910 and 1940, European capitalists used "forced labor regulations" (slavery, that is) to force local farmers off their land to drain rubber trees in the jungle. The Aka were not forced into this slavery. Instead, they primarily became hunters to provide meat for the families of the farmers who couldn't do their own hunting anymore. Their hunting changed to include the net, which caught many more animals, but also depleted the supply of game.

During the 1930s, French colonialists tried to force the Aka to start farming and move onto newly established roads, but the Aka were reluctant to do so. The government stepped in and forced the tribe out of the jungles and gave their land to the timber companies. The Aka were forced to live in villages along the government-built road and stripped of their right to even enter the jungle. The tribespeople, who know the land and have great knowledge of the ecosystem of the Congo, are also forbidden from living in or entering the national parks.

LOOKING AHEAD

Lessened opportunities for hunting have forced many Aka into subsistence farming. Some help neighbors on their coffee plantations. They also do occasional work for local lumber companies and still hunt for legal and illegal bushmeat. A few of the tribe members have been selected to get a Western education, where it is hoped that they will return to their people and help them to adjust to a modern world, one in which they are not allowed to return to their way of life in the jungles.

THE PENAN (SARAWAK IN BORNEO)

The Penan tribe of Sarawak in Borneo have been nomadic jungle hunters for thousands of years. This tribe never practiced agriculture; instead, they depended completely on whatever jungle animals and plants they were able to find for their medicine and food. The outside world knew little of this tribe until the early part of the nineteenth century when it was reported that they were living alongside the Buk and the Hiahm Rivers. The colonial government of Borneo, and the subsequent government of Malaysia, strongly encouraged the Penan to abandon their life as nomads and to settle down in towns.

In the 1950s, Christian missionaries were allowed into the region and began to convert many of the Penan tribe to Protestantism and Catholicism. This period started the Penan's greatest assimilation. Many Penan went to church services on Sunday. They wore Western style clothing, and their children attended government schools.

The Penan settled down on farms to grow bananas, rice, and tapioca once loggers forced them out of the jungle in the 1970s and destroyed their habitat. The Penan lost their major sources of food, their access to rattan palms (used for making baskets and mats) and even access to their ancestral gravesites. It was at this time that they

Logging operations like this one along the Sarawack Rejang river forced the Penan out of the jungle in the 1970s.

were introduced to day labor and a cash economy. Before then, they bartered for what they needed with natural jungle products that they had found. The government of Malaysia insists that they are doing a great favor to the Penans by forcing them to live a more modern existence.

LOOKING AHEAD

Only about ten percent of the remaining Penan still live in the jungles, mountains, and forested areas of the island of Borneo. They are trying to live the way their ancestors did, but the major part of the jungles have been cut due to logging and a booming acacia and oil palm industry, which are grown on large plantations. The fish in the rivers are much reduced because of silt runoff and pollution. The number of animals that the Penan can hunt for food is severely reduced. In addition to these hardships, the government is going ahead with plans to construct twelve hydroelectric dams on

A Few Interesting Facts About The History And Assimilation Of Tribes

When people from Europe began to enter Brazil in the early 1500s, estimates put the population at about 10–11 million indigenous people. During the centuries that followed, colonists brought slave labor, land theft, logging operations, massacres, and disease to the area, so that in the twenty-first century the indigenous population of Brazil is estimated to be less than nine hundred thousand people—or 0.5% of Brazil's population today! Most of these people are now more or less assimilated into modern society, but there still exists a number of small tribes that continue to live deep in the Amazon Jungle; and most of those tribes are found in the western Brazilian state of Acre.

During the latter half of the twentieth century, the Brazilian government attempted to contact these groups and have them join modern society. Their efforts, unfortunately, were unsuccessful and led to government officials and ranchers evicting these people from their land, slaughters, and disease epidemics of devastating proportions. Brazil then decided to create a policy stating that these indigenous groups should be left alone and tried to create protected reserves around them. Protecting these groups is an immense challenge.

Believed to have been stolen more than one hundred years ago from neighboring settlements by an uncontacted Acre tribe, machetes and axes are apparently now part of the tribe's culture.

RESEARCH PROJECT

Choose one of the tribes that are discussed in Chapter 3. Write a paper talking about what you would do if you were part of a government group that has been contacted by a tribe. What would you say to the group about what living in your world is like?

Penan ancestral lands, so the remaining ten percent of Penan tribespeople will have to be relocated. The other ninety percent of Penan have already been resettled on different parts of the island.

TRIBE OF ACRE (BRAZILIAN AMAZON REGION)

The tribe in Acre, Brazil, who were thrust from isolation in August of 2014, stirred up the mainsteam world's interest and concern. This group of more than fifty hunter-gatherers who live in the Brazilian state of Acre's Upper Envira region chose to contact the mainstream world after being threatened by drug traffickers and illegal loggers who entered the area via neighboring Peru. The government of Brazil sent a team of doctors, linguists, and ethnologists to the site of their emergence to prepare and possibly vaccinate them against a set of diseases called the "White Man Flu," which has taken the lives of other newly contacted tribes in the area.

Four tribesmen who made the initial contact with the outsiders started to cough a few days after making contact. These men were immediately **quarantined** and treated by doctors for a respiratory infection. They were treated with antibiotics and then allowed to return to their tribe, promising to return in "one moon's" time. They did not return at that time, but Brazil's agency in charge of the indigenous population, FUNAI, has since set up satellite imaging of the tribe's villages to track their wellness.

UPPER HUMAITA ISOLATED INDIANS (ACRE, BRAZIL)

Another isolated tribe of indigenous people living in the state of Acre, Brazil, have been spotted and were photographed in December 2016 by Ricardo Stuckert, a Brazilian photographer who was flying over the area to photograph other tribes in Acre's jungle. The existence of this tribe has been known for many years; FUNAI calls them the Upper Humaita Isolated Indians. There are historical records showing that this tribe raided settlements back in 1910 and took a number of axes and machetes, which are now an important part of their culture. Those tools allowed them to clear the jungle to create farmland. This group has never chosen to make contact with the outside world, and fortunately look healthy and well fed.

LOOKING AHEAD

Life is becoming increasingly more difficult for the isolated tribes in the Amazon. Resources are becoming scarce, and some of the isolated tribes are staging raids to enter into other tribes' villages and steal whatever they can. Even though it was voted in the 1980s to allow these people to remain uncontacted, the government has recently slashed funding for this project, and has begun to sell lands that were set aside for these tribes to live in the jungle.

TEXT-DEPENDENT QUESTIONS

1. What is the "White Man Flu" and what can be done to treat it?
2. What type of work did the Aka do to survive?
3. Describe the types of costumes the Huli Wigmen wear during their festival dances.

WORDS TO UNDERSTAND

cannibalism – the act of eating human flesh by other human beings

cuscus – a wooly-haired tree-dwelling animal that resembles a monkey that is frequently seen in New Guinea

eco-friendly – earth-friendly; not harmful to Earth's environment

inanimate – not alive like humans and animals; lifeless

CHAPTER 4

A Tribal Way Of Life

All of the jungle tribes that we have covered in the first three chapters are unique in some way and practice some very interesting traditions and behaviors.

THE PENAN TRIBE OF SARAWAK IN BORNEO

The Penan people of Borneo never practiced agriculture until they were forced to, after World War II. In fact, they were one of the last tribes in the world who were strictly hunter-gatherers. Deep in the jungles of Sarawak, Penans can still be found roaming the jungle, gathering food to eat and hunting for deer and wild boar with blowguns. Blowguns are simple weapons that are made from sections of thick bamboo formed into small tubes, frequently decorated with a carving of a woman with extremely long earlobes. The darts that are blown through the tubes are cut from thinner bamboo sticks, of which one end is dipped into a poison called tajem, which is made from latex extracted from a certain tree bark that paralyzes and kills their prey.

The Penan also catch fish in the many nearby rivers. Their main traditional food is sago, a starchy foodstuff that is found in the center of trunks of certain palm trees. This foodstuff is scraped out, washed thoroughly, and then dried to make flour, which

The Penan still use blowguns, sections of thick bamboo formed into small tubes, and poison-tipped darts to hunt.

can be rolled into balls and mixed with boiling water to make an edible pancake. They also eat jungle fruits and plants, frogs, lizards, certain insects, and snails. Most Penan still rely on certain jungle plants for their medicine.

The Penan language belongs to the Austronesian language family, which includes languages spoken in Indonesia, Borneo, the Philippines, Taiwan, Vietnam, Oceania, and Madagascar. The Penan people have always lived an **eco-friendly** existence. They still practice traditional values, such as sharing everything equally (the failure to share is their biggest misdeed). Their concept of "molong" is a belief that all animals and jungle plants should be used and harvested responsibly. They will never take more than is necessary, and they will replant to preserve food for future generations.

Before the Christian missionaries converted most of the Penan to Christianity (starting in the 1930s), they believed in animism, which is the belief that all plants, animals, thunder, and even rocks and other **inanimate** objects are interconnected and have a soul. They believe humans have two souls, one that is emotional and physical, and the other one that wanders the world in a dreamlike state. They also believed in a supernatural power or god called Peselong, who created and organized the world. Medicine men or women called shamans can cure most illnesses by removing spirits that are causing the illness from the body.

One unusual belief that the Penan had was that women were thought to be born without souls, and would only get a soul when they married. Before they got a soul, they could act wild and carefree; but after marriage, they must settle down and have children.

THE AKA TRIBE OF CENTRAL AFRICA

The Aka tribe of the Congo Republic and the Central African Republic are a traditional society of hunter-gatherers that has only recently started to plant their own crops instead of trading for food with other neighboring villages. Many Aka still trade forest products like bushmeat and honey for plantains, yams, taro, corn, squash, papayas, pineapples, rice, and palm oils.

The Aka people speak a musical sounding language called Diaka, which has three different tones. Depending on the tone used, for example, the word *mbongo* can mean a panther, a kind of bee, or a cup! They also speak two other languages: Sango (also known as Ngbandi), which is an Ubangian language and the national language of the Central African Republic, and Bantu, which is spoken by their village trading partners. The Aka have a very complex type of music, which involves much

The Aka have a very complex type of music, which involves much chanting and community improvisation.

chanting and community improvisation. Some Aka girls and women also perform water drumming, or liquindi. They stand in the water and then use their hands to hit the water in a certain way to make a sound like drumming.

The Aka roam over a very large territory, and there are different religious beliefs in each area. Some of the Aka believe in a creator of all things called Bembe, but they also believe that Bembe retired for good after the hard work of creation. Other Aka believe in Djengi, who is a helpful, powerful jungle spirit. Aka who wish to communicate with Djengi go to a tuma, or traditional healer, who knows how to translate Djengi's supernatural language. Other healers called Ngangas are believed to cure illnesses, tell the Aka exactly where in the jungle to find game animals, can see ahead to the future, and help people to make life decisions. The Aka do not believe in a heaven. They believe that the spirits of their dead family members stick around on Earth, visiting their family, and frequently wanting and asking for things.

The Aka have a very warm and loving family life. Both women and men provide food for the family equally, and either the wife or husband can start divorce proceedings. Violence against women is almost unheard of, and there has never been an incident of rape reported among the Aka. Aka fathers are considered to be among the best fathers in the world. They play a very active role in their children's lives and hold their young

The Aka have warm and loving family lives. Babies are never unattended, but rather held constantly.

children close to them for hours on end. In fact, a baby is never left lying unattended—they are held constantly. The Aka believe that there is nothing in this world more precious than children, and so children are always treated with great affection and love.

HULI WIGMEN OF PAPUA NEW GUINEA

The Huli Wigmen live in the southern Highlands and Hela Province of Papua New Guinea. There is no brighter, more colorful tribe in Papua New Guinea than the famous Huli Wigmen. They wear brilliant headdresses made from the colorful, ginger-red feathers of the Raggiana bird-of-paradise. They paint their faces in bright colors as soon as they reach adulthood. But by far the most interesting thing about the Huli Wigmen's attire is their carefully grown and cultivated hair, which is made into fantastic wigs containing flowers, ornaments, bird feathers, and different colors of pigment.

Observe the craftsmanship of the Huli people.

Some boys leave their village at fourteen years old (leaving the women to do all the gardening and agriculture) and go to a special area of the jungle where they are taught to grow wigs and prove their manhood by learning special hunting techniques. The price of admission into the school is one pig (pigs are domesticated animals of the Huli, and are seldom, if ever, eaten for meat). A wig used for everyday activities takes about eighteen months to grow, and a ceremonial wig takes thirty-six months. The boys learn how to grow their hair, how to sprinkle "magic water" over their wigs so the hair will be perfect, and they also learn other forms of spiritual cleansing. Some boys stay in this area and grow wigs back to back for about ten years, or until they wish to return home and marry.

A Growing Concern

There are several different theories as to why the Aka people and other pygmy tribes are so short. Some scientists say that their short height evolved because the leaves of the trees allowed less ultraviolet light to enter the jungle, so the skin of the people who lived there would produce less vitamin D. Vitamin D is necessary for the body to absorb calcium, which makes bones grow. The less calcium that is absorbed, the smaller skeletons and bones become.

Other research shows that being smaller might make it easier to move around in thick jungle; it could also be because less food exists in a jungle environment, so the inhabitants did not grow as big as others. Over the generations, because height is hereditary, the Aka's lack of height passed from parents to the children in their genes.

Foreigners who first met up with the Huli tribespeople were told that they were cannibals, and this tale kept many unwanted visitors (especially missionaries) away over the years. The truth is that the story of **cannibalism** is just a myth. Huli men are people with a great sense of fun, but they do

At celebrations known as sing sings, the Huli paint their bodies and wear their colorful wigs.

frequently have battles with other tribesmen over relatively minor things. They indulge in three major types of disputes—they fight over pigs (which are used as money and as symbols of wealth), women, and land. A Huli male needs land for farming, one or more wives to take care of the homestead, and pigs to demonstrate his wealth.

There are many other interesting facts about the Huli tribespeople. Women are the chief food growers and provide the Huli with yams, manioc (also known as cassava), and other foods. Pork is sometimes eaten on special occasions, but pigs are used primarily for trade and shows of wealth. Wild cassowary, **cuscus**, and tree kangaroos are hunted for meat.

The Huli live in round grass roofed and mud-walled huts. Traditionally the men slept in one hut, and the pigs and women slept in another, but the missionaries discouraged this practice, and nowadays most villagers have a third hut for their pigs. Traditional outfits include grass skirts for the women and kotecas and string aprons for the men. Frequent celebrations are held called sing-sings where men get to wear their traditional colorful wigs and paint their bodies.

RESEARCH PROJECT

After reading about the spiritual traditions of many jungle tribes, write a report on what is the role of the medicine man or shaman in these cultures.

TRIBES OF ACRE (BRAZILIAN AMAZON REGION)

For the few indigenous tribes of the Amazonian rainforest that are still able to live in the jungle, life is very similar to the lives led by their ancestors thousands of years ago. Hunting and fishing (fish, capybara, crocodiles, and turtles) are a very important part of their lives, as is hunting for plants, wild fruits, and nuts, which are used for both food and medicine in the jungle. Blowguns and poison darts were used for thousands of years for hunting, but have mostly been replaced with more modern weapons like guns. Small garden plots are kept to grow other food, like papaya, banana plants, peanuts, and manioc. Children do not go to school; instead, their elders teach them how to survive in the jungle.

The spirit world is widely respected by Acre's indigenous peoples, and they frequently use hallucinogenic plants that allow them to get closer to the world of the supernatural. Most jungle tribes in the Amazon have a healer called a shaman who knows how to perform rites, communicate with spirits, and use local animals and plants to make medicines and ointments.

Acre-based tribes speak many languages, from modern to ancient. These include Panoan, Portuguese, Arawakan, Ashaninka, Tupi-Guarani, Arawá, and Maipurean.

Crocodiles are among the animals that Acre tribes hunt to feed their families.

TEXT-DEPENDENT QUESTIONS

1. What are pigs used for in the Huli culture?
2. What role does an Aka father play in the lives of his children?
3. What is water drumming, as performed by Aka women?

WORDS TO UNDERSTAND

annihilated – utterly and completely destroyed

decimating – destroying, killing, or removing a large part of something

longhouses – long communal dwellings constructed of wood and bark

mahogany – a tropical tree with hard reddish-brown wood that is popular for making high-quality furniture

squatter – a person who occupies land or a building that is uninhabited unlawfully

subsidiary – one company that is controlled or owned by another company

CHAPTER 5

The Dangers Of The Modern World

The modern world is a hostile and very dangerous place for tribes who, either by choice or circumstance, live apart from other people in this world and maintain their traditional lives in the jungle. This chapter will talk about the very real threats that tribes are facing in the twenty-first century—threats that could completely destroy the continued existence of these groups of people as jungle tribes.

TRIBES OF THE AMAZON

The many Amazonian Jungle tribes, including the tribes living in the state of Acre, Brazil, are faced with a multitude of threats that are impacting their very existence. The Akuntsu tribe of Brazil were almost completely **annihilated** in the 1990s because of ruthless cattle ranchers who took their lands, cut down their jungle home, killed almost all of the tribe, and then tried to cover up their deeds by bulldozing the houses of the tribe to pretend that they had never lived there. Today only five members of this tribe exist.

Everyday, more and more of the Amazon Jungle is destroyed.

Fifty percent of the Nahua Indians of the Peruvian Amazon died from introduced diseases like measles, chicken pox, and influenza (flu) after their lands were destroyed by companies exploring for oil on their lands in the 1980s. Half of the Murunahua tribe also died from diseases in the 1990s after illegal **mahogany** loggers forcibly contacted them.

After more than five hundred years, Christian missionaries—whose general purpose is to actively promote conversion to Christianity because they believe it is the only religion that has God's approval —are still trying to force themselves into the lives of rarely contacted jungle tribes. These conversion attempts are often made regardless of the wishes of the people and sometimes at the cost of the tribespeople's health. In the 1980s, a fundamentalist Christian group was determined to contact and convert the Zo'é tribe of Brazil. The missionaries flew over the remote villages dropping "gifts," and then constructed a mission station a few day's walk from the village. After the missionaries finally made contact in 1987, forty-five members of the Zo'é tribe died from malaria and flu epidemics, as well as respiratory diseases that were all transmitted by the insistent missionaries.

Illegal loggers are invading the lands of uncontacted tribes in the Peruvian Amazon. The loggers are after some of the jungle's last stands of mahogany trees, which bring a large amount of money in the mainstream world. These loggers destroyed the Murunahua tribe back in the 1980s, and are currently destroying the Maschco Piro tribe. The tribespeople try to run away but are chased down and shot and killed by these ruthless loggers.

Road builders bulldozed the land of the Brazilian Panará tribe in the 1970s. The builders introduced the natives to alcohol, and four-fifths of the tribe died of disease or were killed in a span of just eight short years.

The Amazon and other jungles are being destroyed so that lucrative palm-tree plantations like this one in Brazil can be planted.

The birds of paradise, whose feathers adorn Huli wigs, have all but disappeared in Papua New Guinea due to the destruction of their habitat.

HULI TRIBE OF PAPUA NEW GUINEA

The natural habitat of the Huli tribe is being lost at an incredible rate. The outside world is encroaching on the tribal lands, by mining, logging, capturing and then selling wildlife, and by converting all the surrounding land areas to farming, particularly of palm oil trees. The jungle is being destroyed so that large plantations of palm trees can be planted, and the open cast mines that are being built are polluting and **decimating** the rivers and jungles of Papua New Guinea at an alarming rate.

Seventy percent of the island of Papua New Guinea is still covered with jungle, in third place after the Congo basin and Amazonia. It is a rich ecosystem that must be protected. In the ten years between 1998 and 2008 alone, two hundred eighteen new plants and more than one thousand new species were discovered there. The Huli are threatened by deforestation, which means that outsiders are cutting down part of their jungle for the valuable wood that grows there. Deforestation also means that there is less space for wild animals to live so that the Huli are not able to find enough meat by hunting. Another sad reality is that the birds-of-paradise whose feathers are used to decorate the Hulu wigs are now almost completely gone from the island since their habitat has been destroyed.

In 2014, a **subsidiary** of Exxon-Mobile called PNG LNG (Papua New Guinea Liquified Natural-Gas) began to extract gas from the Huli Highlands and transport it by pipeline to the capital, Port Moresby. The company promised the Huli people new land and profit sharing if they sold their land to the company cheaply. Now new roads, airports,

Wigging Out

The word Papua probably comes from the Malay word Papuwah, which means "fuzzy hair." This means that the tradition of growing fantastic wig hair by Huli males has been around for a very long time. Despite the fact that some Huli Wigmen still go into the jungle and learn how to grow the beautiful wigs and love to perform in village demonstrations called sing-sings, there are many changes happening in the Huli culture in the twenty-first century.

For example, many Huli and beginning to wear mostly Western style clothing as their everyday dress. The traditional dress is now reserved for special occasions and for tourists. The Huli used to yodel back and forth across the mountains. Now that the cell phone has been introduced, you can no longer hear any yodeling. Finally, the number of boys who go into the jungle to grow the fabulous Huli wigs has decreased drastically.

The Baka are among the African jungle tribes that have been forcibly displaced from their land.

and processing facilities have been built and the gas is being removed, but the Huli have seen few benefits and promised infrastructure and economic improvements have not been delivered.

There is another major threat that the modern world has brought to the tribes of Papua New Guinea—guns, including semi-automatic pistols. The tribespeople traditionally have engaged in occasional tribal fighting using spears and bows and arrows. Unfortunately, high-powered weapons make these conflicts much more deadly.

THE AKA AND OTHER TRIBES OF CENTRAL AFRICA

The Aka tribe, as well as the Baka, Twa, and Mbuti people who live in the Democratic Republic of Congo (DRC) and the Central African Republic (CAR) are being threatened by conservation projects that have displaced them from their lands, and the jungles are being degraded by illegal expansion by neighboring farmers over-logging and over-trading of bushmeat. The Aka have not received any type of compensation for their lands and loss of livelihood, and many are forced to live in "**squatter**" settlements outside the land that once belonged to them, where they suffer from poor health and severe levels of poverty.

The African governments never recognized that the Aka and other tribes had any rights to the land, so it was sold right out from under them. Not only has their land been stolen, but groups of armed militia have beaten, assaulted, and even killed them. They became sick and no longer had access to their traditional jungle medicines. There is

RESEARCH PROJECT

After reading this book and watching the videos that are recommended, write a paper talking about your opinion on contacting previously uncontacted jungle tribes. Should they be left alone? Should they be assimilated into the world outside the jungle?

When jungles are destroyed, plants, trees, animals and insects disappear with them.

also racism; white people who have acquired land taken by force from native tribes then pay the black tribespeople very little to work the new farms and companies built on that land.

Multinational logging companies are extracting whatever valuable timber remains in the jungle. A 2014 study published by the National Academy of Sciences concluded that in areas of the Amazon affected by deforestation, the incidence of sicknesses including respiratory infection and malaria increases more than 40%. As a result, the Aka are dying at an alarming rate since they have no money to pay for medicine and no access to the jungle for their traditional medicines. Some of the governments of Central Africa are happy to evict the Aka from their habitat because they want to make money from selling the valuable hardwood trees and from selling the cleared land to corporations and farmers from other parts of the country. Their greed for profit today is very dangerous for the ecological health of the world. When jungles or rainforests are destroyed many animals, insects, and plants become extinct.

There are reports that, during the Congo Civil War in 2003, the Aka were hunted down by their enemies and eaten like game animals. The organization Minority Rights Group International has testified to the UN Security Council that there is substantial evidence of cannibalism, mass killings, and rape of the Aka and other tribes.

THE PENAN OF SARAWAK, BORNEO, AND OTHER NEIGHBORING TRIBES

A small portion of the Penan tribe has been relocated into the Gunung Mulu National Park in Sarawak, Borneo, which is about ninety percent closed to outside visitors. However, the Penan still suffer from outsiders practicing illegal activities in the park, like hunting the wild boars, which takes away the Penan's main source of meat.

Areas of land on the border of the National Park have been heavily cut and logged, so much so that the ecosystem of the land within the park borders is threatened. There is a great deal of soil erosion caused by logging and jungle conversion and industrial palm oil plantations, which is affecting the waterways of the park. Open pit mines and burned scrub lands also contribute to the destruction of the habitat.

The Penan who do not live within the borders of the park have been settled into longhouses with access to electricity. The younger members of the tribe are sitting around watching TV and using their cell phones and aren't receiving any of the traditional lessons of their people, like the names of one thousand five hundred of the most common trees, or the myths about the origin of animals and humans. These Penan are now evangelical Protestants because of the missionaries who encroached on their territory years ago. Some of these Penan are even working for the oil-palm growers and logging companies that destroyed their jungle and their traditional way of life.

This longhouse is home to Orang Ulu tribe members, also of the Sarawak of the Bornean jungle. These homes have a very distinctive architecture style, elevated upon tall wooden stilts, decorated with tribal paintings in plant and animal motifs, long open airy verandas and large rooms for communal living. One such large longhouse can accommodate a whole small village or a community of villagers.

The Penan hunt wild boar, or bearded pigs, but poaching on their lands has dwindled the boar population and reduced the Penan's food supply.

TEXT-DEPENDENT QUESTIONS

1. What are some of the reasons why the Aka tribe has been driven out of their traditional lands?

2. Why do missionaries want to bring their religion to uncontacted tribes, and what is one of the results of people from the outside world making contact with tribes for the first time?

3. What differences are there in the life of the Penan who live in a national park and the Penans who live outside of the park?

SERIES GLOSSARY OF KEY TERMS

Assimilation - The process by which a person or persons acquire the social and psychological characteristics of a group or society

Canopy - Also called crown canopy or crown cover, this refers to the cover formed by the leafy upper branches of the trees in a forest

Carnivorous - subsisting or feeding on animal tissues, or in the case of some plants, subsisting on nutrients obtained from the breakdown of animal protoplasm

Colonialism - control by one country over another area and its people

Conservation - a careful preservation and protection of something, such as the planned management of a natural resource to prevent exploitation, destruction, or neglect

Creature – an animal of any type

Culture – the customary beliefs, social forms, and material traits of a racial, religious, or social group, and the characteristic features of everyday existence (such as diversions or a way of life) shared by the people of those groups in a place or time

Deforestation – the action or process of the clearing of forests through cutting or burning its trees

Enzymes - any of numerous complex proteins that are produced by living cells and catalyze specific natural biochemical reactions at body temperatures, such as digestion

Habitat - the place or environment where a plant or animal naturally or normally lives and grows

Indigenous - produced, growing, living, or occurring naturally in a particular region or environment

Nocturnal - active at night

Oxygen - a reactive element that is found in water, in most rocks and minerals, in numerous organic compounds, and as a colorless tasteless odorless diatomic gas constituting 21 percent of the atmosphere, that is capable of combining with all elements except the inert gases and is active in physiological processes; estimates say that trees of the world's jungles produce 30 to 55 percent of the oxygen in the atmosphere

Parasite - an animal, insect or plant that lives in or on another animal or plant and gets food or protection from it

Poaching – to trespass on land for the purpose of taking fish or game illegally

Predator - an animal that lives by killing and eating other animals

Rainforest - a tropical woodland with an annual rainfall of at least 100 inches (254 centimeters) and marked by lofty broad-leaved evergreen trees forming a continuous canopy

Species - a category of biological classification ranking immediately below the genus or subgenus, comprising related organisms or populations potentially capable of inter-breeding, and being designated by a common name

Tropical - of, being, or characteristic of a region or climate that is frost-free with temperatures high enough to support year-round plant growth given sufficient moisture

Venom - a toxic substance produced by some animals (such as snakes, scorpions, or bees) that is injected into prey or an enemy chiefly by biting or stinging and has an injurious or lethal effect

DOCUMENTARIES

The Jungle of the Red Spirit, 2012

The jungles of Borneo are especially famous for the enormous number of species of the most sophisticated flower in the world—the Orchid. In this documentary, viewers will see the beauty close-up as they climb the tree trunks of this beautiful jungle guided by the "man of the forest."

The Sacred Science, 2011

In October of 2010, eight people, suffering from various illnesses, chose to leave everything behind and spend thirty days in a corner of the world that is home to a vanishing group of indigenous healers in uncharted regions of the Amazon rainforest. Five would come back with real results, two would come back disappointed, and one wouldn't come back at all. This is their story.

Swamp Tigers, 2001

This documentary takes a look at one of the most efficient predators on Earth. Cameraman Mike Herd captured the legendary swamp tiger on film for the first time years ago. It was an extraordinary breakthrough, the first glimpse into the secret life of the least known tiger in the world - the swamp tiger of the Bangladeshi Sundarbans.

Further Reading

Arkus, Michael. *Bussing The Amazon: On The Road With The Accidental Journalist*. Seattle: CreateSpace On-Demand Publishing LLC (Amazon), 2014.

Beccari, Odoardo. *Wanderings In The Great Forests Of Borneo: Travels And Researches Of A Naturalist In Sarawak* (Kindle Edition). Seattle: Amazon Digital Services LLC, 2015.

Beehler, Bruce M. *Lost Worlds: Adventures In The Tropical Rainforest*. New Haven: Yale University Press, 2008.

Corazza, Lago. *The Last Men: Journey Among The Tribes Of New Guinea*. New Zealand: White Star Publishers, 2010.

Frederiksen, Henrik. *We Drifted Into The Amazon: A Homemade Bamboo Raft Down The Mighty Amazon River*, Unsupported (Kindle Edition). Seattle: Amazon Digital Services LLC, 2015.

Hewlett, Bonnie L. *Listen, Here Is A Story: Ethnographic Life Narratives From Aka And Ngandu Women Of The Congo Basin*. Oxford: Oxford University Press, 2012.

Internet Resources

https://www.worldwildlife.org/places/congo-basin
This excellent website discussing ethnic groups in the Congo Basin is maintained and updated by the World Wildlife Fund (WWF), the world's foremost conservation organization.

http://thinkjungle.com/amazon-rainforest-tribes/
This excellent page on Amazon Rainforest tribes is maintained by ThinkJungle.com, an organization that provides Amazonian rainforest tours.

http://www.survivalinternational.org/tribes/pygmies
Survival International, a global organization that defends tribal peoples' rights around the world. This webpage focuses on news concerning the Aka tribe, among others, who live in the rainforests of Central Africa.

http://www.bbc.com/future/story/20140804-sad-truth-of-uncontacted-tribes
This website created and maintained by BBC News provides updates and history concerning so-called uncontacted tribes around the globe.

https://data.mongabay.com/borneo/borneo_people.html
Mongabay.com provides "News and Inspiration from Nature's Frontline." This page contains many interesting facts about the people and tribes of Borneo.

http://www.independent.co.uk/news/science/new-guinea-indigenous-tribes-dani-people-bbc-documentary-mistakes-ancient-people-amputation-a7690506.html
The Independent is an online newspaper with a US edition and a UK edition. They frequently cover news about Papua New Guinea, including this interesting page about Papua New Guinea's indigenous tribes.

Educational Video Links

Chapter 1: http://x-qr.net/1DV1

Take a look at an example of how life has changed for the Penan.

Chapter 2: http://x-qr.net/1Esi

Very little is known about the so-called Sentinelese people, who live in isolation in the Indian Ocean.

Chapter 3: http://x-qr.net/1F0n

Aka tribeswomen are joyous at the conclusion of a successful hunt.

Chapter 4: http://x-qr.net/1FZh

Observe the craftsmanship of the Huli people.

Chapter 5: http://x-qr.net/1GcW

Everyday, more and more of the Amazon Jungle is destroyed.

INDEX

A

Acre Tribes (Amazon, Brazil), 11–13, 26–27, 26–30, 44–45
    companies effect on, 42
    diet, 16, 56–57, **57**
    diseases and medicines, 42, 56
    education in, 56
    farming by, 56
    first contact of, 26–27
    government involvement, 42, 44, 45
    land protection for, 42, 45
    languages in, 56
    location on world map, 6
    Macaw People, 26–27
    religious beliefs, 56
    relocation of, 42
    slavery, 42
    Upper Envira region group, 44
    Upper Humaita Isolated Indians, 44–45
    violence against, 42
    way of life, 16, 42, 56–57
    weapons, 43, **43,** 56
    Xatanawa, 26–27
activists and environmentalists, 21
African tribes. See Aka of Central Africa
agricultural companies, 12
Aka of Central Africa, 15–18, 38–40, **50**
    assimilation, 15, 40
    as cannibalism victims, 67
    companies effect on, 17, 18, 39, 68
    diet of, 15, 18, 49
    diseases and medicines, 50, 65
    drumming, 50
    fathers' behavior in, 17, 51
    first contact, 24–26, 25
    government involvement with, 38, 39, 67
    habitat destruction, 68
    hunter-gatherers, **16,** 17, 18, 25, 38, 39, 49
    land rights and compensation, 65
    languages, 49
    location on world map, 6
    Mbenga pygmy people, 15, 17, 25
    money and work, 18, 39
    music by, 17
    'pygmies of Darkest Africa,' 17, 25
    religious beliefs, 50–51
    relocation of, 40, 65
    Schweinfurth, Georg August, 25, 26
    slavery, 15, 17, 25, 26
    threats to, 64–67
    UN Security Council on killings of, 67
    video of, 39
    violence suffered by, 25, 67
    way of life of, 17, 18, **38,** 49–52, 51
    websites about, 74
    Western education by, 40
Akuntsu tribe of Brazil, 59
Amazon tribes, 6, 16, 72, 74. See also Acre Tribes (Amazon, Brazil)
Asháninka people, 26–27
assimilation of indigenous people, 28–30, 40, 42
Aztecs (Mexico), diseases from first contact, 33

B

Bayaka of Central Africa, 26, 38–40, **64,** 65. See also Aka of Central Africa
Borneo tribes. See Penan people of Sarawak of Borneo
Bose Yacu, 30
Brazil tribes. See Acre Tribes (Amazon, Brazil)

C
cannibalism, 53, 67
companies
    agriculture, 16
    farmers, 65, 67
    gas, 63–64
    logging (See logging companies)
    oil, 12, 32, 60
    plantations (See plantations)
    ranchers, 12, 42, 59
compensation to tribes, 65
Congo, location on world map, 6
Congolese tribes. See Aka of Central Africa
conservation of the jungle, 62–63, 65
Cujareño people (Amazon, Peru), 27–28

D
definitions, 10, 22, 34, 46, 58
deforestation, 12, 16, 19, 62, 63, 66, 67
diseases and medicines
    Acre Tribes (Amazon, Brazil), 42, 44, 56
    Asháninka, 27
    Aztecs (Mexico), 33
    deforestation effect on, 67
    first contact and, 32–33
    Incas (Peru), 33
    missionaries, 60
    Murunahua tribe (Brazil Amazon), 60
    Nahua Indians of the Peruvian Amazon, 60
    Upper Envira region tribe, 44
    "White Man Flu," 44
    Zo'é tribe of Brazil, 60–61
documentaries, 72
drug traffickers, Xatanawa first contact, 26–27

E
ecosystem knowledge, 39
education, 13, 40, 53, 56
Europeans, 18, 42

F
farmers, 16, 65, 67
first contact issues, 22–34
    Asháninka, 27
    Aztecs (Mexico), 33
    Incas (Peru), 33
    interpreters, 26
    Mashco Piro Tribe (Amazon, Peru), 27–28

    Miani, Giovanni, 26
    need for allies and weapons, 27
    Sentinelese Tribe (India), 30
    sicknesses, 27
    uncontacted tribes, 44
    Upper Envira region group (Amazon, Brazil), 44
    Xatanawa, 26–27
Fox, Jack and Tom, 23, 24
FUNAI, 11, 26–27, 44, 46
Fundaçao Nacional do Índio (FUNAI), 11, 26–27, 44, 46

G
genocide. See violence
government involvement
    Acre Tribes (Amazon, Brazil), 42, 44, 45
    Aka of Central Africa, 38, 39, 67
    land rights and policies, 13, 65
    medical treatments of Acre Tribes, 44
    profit from jungles, 67
    relocation of Ruc Tribe, 31
    Sentinelese Tribe (India), 30
    violence prevention between tribes, 28
    Yawanawa people, 13

H
history books inaccuracies, 24
Huli Wigmen of Papua New Guinea, 13–15, **34,** 35–37
    agriculture, 36
    assimilation of, 35–36, 37
    Bird Dance, 15
    birds-of-paradise and, 63
    clothing, 36, 55
    companies, 37, 62, 63–64
    conflicts within, 55
    diet, 23, **36,** 37, 55, 63
    education, 13, 53
    farming by, 37, 55
    festivals and shows, 14, 15, 35–36, **37, 54,** 55
    first contact, 23–24, 36
    habitat destruction, 62, 63–64
    Highland civilization and, 13
    Leahy brothers and, 35
    pigs as symbol of wealth, 15, 55
    traditional costume of, **14,** 15, **37,** 52, **54,** 61, **62**
    way of life, 15, 36, 52–55
    weapons, 37, 64
    wigs made by, 13, 15, 35–36, 52, 53, **54, 62,** 63

I

icons described, 5
illnesses. See diseases and medicines
Incas (Peru), 33
indigenous jungle peoples, 8–9
isolated tribes. See uncontacted tribes

J

jungle destruction. See deforestation

K

key icons, 5

L

land protection, 42, 45
Leahy, Dan and Mick, 23, 35
logging companies
    Acre Tribes (Amazon, Brazil), 42
    Aka of Central Africa, 39, 68
    conservation of the jungle, 12
    encroachment of jungle tribes, 16
    habitat degradation by, 65
    Huli Wigmen of Papua New Guinea, 63
    Mashco Piro Tribe (Amazon, Peru), 61
    Murunahua tribe (Brazil Amazon), 60–61
    Pacahuara Tribe (Bolivia), 28
    Penan people of Sarawak of Borneo, 19, 40, 41, **41**
    racism by, 67
    slavery, 32
    violence, 32, 61
    Xatanawa first contact, 26–27

M

Macaw People, 26–27
map of the world, 6–7
Mashco Piro Tribe (Amazon, Peru), 27–28, 61
Mbenga pygmy people, 15, 17, 25
Mbuti of Central Africa, 65
Miani, Giovanni, 26
mining companies
    Aka of Central Africa, 68
    conservation of the jungle, 12
    encroachment of jungle tribes, 16
    first contact, 23, 24
    gold panning, **24**
    Huli Wigmen of Papua New Guinea, 62
    racism by, 67
    slavery, 32

violence, 23, 24, 32
Minority Rights Group International, 67
missionaries, 27, 32, 40, 49, 53, 55, 60–61
Murunahua tribe (Brazil Amazon), 60–61

N

Nahua Indians of the Peruvian Amazon, 60
National Academy of Sciences studies, 67
Nomole people (Amazon, Peru), 27–28, 61

O

oil companies, 12, 32, 60
Orang Ulu tribe, 68, **68**

P

Pacahuara Tribe (Bolivia), 28–30, **29**
palm oil and acacia plantations, 21
Panará tribe of Brazil, 61
Papua New Guinea indigenous tribes. See Penan People of Sarawak of Borneo
Papua New Guinea Liquified Natural-Gas (PNG LNG), 63–64
Penan people of Sarawak of Borneo, 18–21, 47–49
    activists and environmentalists, 21
    agriculture transition, 40, 47
    assimilation, 40
    blowguns, 19, 47, **48**
    deforestation, 19, 21, 40, 41
    diet, 18–19, 21, 40, 41, 47–48, 67, **68**
    education of children, 40
    electricity use by, 68
    government involvement, 19, 21, 41, 44
    homes, 21, 68, **68**
    hunter-gatherers, 18–19, **20,** 47
    hydroelectric projects effect on, 21, 41, 44
    illegal hunting effects on, 67
    language, 48
    location on world map, 7
    logging effect on, 19, 40, 41, **41**
    medicine from the jungle, 19, 48, 49
    money and work, 40–41, 68
    plantations in jungle and, 19, 21, 41
    religious beliefs, 19, 40, 48, 49, 68
    relocation of, 21, 44, 67, 68
    threats to, 67–69
    way of life, 17, 18, 19, 21, 40, 47–49, 48, 72
    websites about, 74

Phong Nha-Ke Bang National Park (Vietnam) and Ruc tribe, 31
plantations
    acacia and palm oil, 21
    Aka of Central Africa, 18, 68
    coffee, 17, 18, 40
    Huli Wigmen of Papua New Guinea, 62
    palm oil and acacia, 21, 41, **61,** 62, 68
    Penan people of Sarawak of Borneo, 19, 21, 41
    rubber, 17, 27, 28, 32, 39
plants discovered, 62–63
PNG LNG (Papua New Guinea Liquified Natural-Gas), 63–64
pygmies, 15, 17, 25

Q
QR codes, 18, 32, 39, 52, 60, 75
questions, 21, 33, 45, 57, 69

R
relocation of tribes, 21, 31, 40, 44, 65, 67, 68
rescue vs invasion, 28–30
research project, 19
rights activists, 8, 29
road builders, Panará tribe of Brazil affected by, 61
Ruc tribe (Vietnam), 31

S
Schweinfurth, Georg August, **25,** 26, 38
Sentinelese Tribe (India), 30, 32
SIL International (Summer Institute of Linguistics), 28–30
slavery, 15, 17, 25, 26, 27–28
Stanley, Henry Morton, **25**
Stuckert, Ricardo, 44
Summer Institute of Linguistics (SIL International), 28–30
Sundarbans Reserve, location on world map, 7

T
Tari, Highlands of, 13
threats to jungle tribes, 58–69
Twa of Central Africa, 65

U
uncontacted tribes
    in Acre, Brazil, 11–12, 26–27
    in the Amazon jungle, 12
    benefits and challenges of contact, 9, 11
    companies and, 9
    diseases after first contact, 32–33

governments and, 9
    number of, 11
    Pacahuara Tribe (Bolivia), 28
    Papua New Guinea, 31
    protection measures, 11
    websites about, 74
    See also diseases and medicines; first contact issues
UNESCO World Heritage Site, 7
UN Security Council and Aka of Central Africa killings, 67
Upper Envira region tribe, 44
Upper Humaita Isolated Indians, 45

V
videos, 18, 32, 39, 52, 60, 75
village along the Amazon, **12**
violence
    Acre Tribes (Amazon, Brazil), 42
    Aka of Central Africa, 25, 67
    Akuntsu tribe of Brazil, 59
    genocide of indigenous people, 13
    government prevention of, 28
    trading vs, 23, 24

W
way of life of jungle tribes, 46–57
weapons, 19, 27, 37, 43, 47, 56, 64
website links, 74
words to understand, 10, 22, 34, 46, 58

X
Xatanawa, 26–27
Yawanawa people, 13

Z
Zo'é tribe of Brazil, 60–61

ABOUT THE AUTHOR

Lori is a graduate of the University of Pittsburgh and has traveled all over Central and

South America. She loves books, learning, music, traveling, and new opportunities.

Since an early age, she has written articles for newspapers and magazines. For more

than a decade, she has been an editorial and design judge for the Benjamin Franklin

Publishing Awards. As a cataloger in a large university library, she created thousands

of bibliographic records detailing content and subject headings of books. She is also a

prolific blogger known for her thoughtful writing, as well as her keen sense of humor.

To top it all off, Lori is fluent in Spanish.